Starters

MAXINE CLARK

D1313153

Contents

Managing Editor: Janet Illsley
Photographer: David Gill
Designer: Sue Storey
Food Stylist: Maxine Clark
Photographic Stylist: Maria Jacques
Typeset by Angel Graphics
Colour separation by Fotographics, UK - Hong Kong
Printed in Italy by New Interlitho S.p.A.

Published 1991 by Merehurst Ltd,
Ferry House, 51/57 Lacy Rd, Putney, London SW15 1PR

© Merehurst Ltd

ISBN: 1 85391 180 1 (Cased)
ISBN: 1 85391 265 4 (Paperback)

A catalogue record for this book is available from the British Library.

NOTES
All spoon measures are level: 1 tablespoon = 15ml spoon;
1 teaspoon = 5ml spoon.
Use fresh herbs and freshly ground black pepper unless
otherwise stated.

Introduction

Choosing a starter in a restaurant is difficult at the best of times. Selecting a starter to serve at your own dinner party usually presents the same problem. When planning a dinner, I tend to think of a main course first, then build the rest of the meal around it. This way you can choose food complementary to the central dish.

A starter should never be too heavy, too large or too rich. It is meant to whet the appetite for what is to follow, not to dull the palate and kill the appetite! Avoid filling everyone up with too many nibbles before the meal, or your carefully chosen starter won't be appreciated, never mind the main course! Try to create a balance of flavours and textures throughout the meal without having, say fruit, fish, cream, or pastry in every course.

If you are likely to be pushed for time, make the starter well ahead. You could create drama with a soufflé prepared in advance and popped in the oven as you have pre-dinner drinks!

Why not serve a meal entirely composed of starters – my sister's dream meal! The Turks and Greeks have been doing it for centuries in their 'mezze'. Many of the recipes in this book – such as chicken livers with polenta, pepper and garlic pizzette and mouclade – can be eaten as a main course if you double the quantities.

This is very much a collection of my favourite starters, derived from my travels, dinners with friends, discussions with fellow cooks, and meals in restaurants. Now that we have such a variety and quality of ingredients in this country, there is no excuse for a limp prawn cocktail, or a tasteless melon with a glacé cherry on top – the world is your oyster! I hope you enjoy using this book and adding your own touches to the recipes.

Maxine A. Clark

Mosaic Vegetable Terrine

This colourful starter tastes rather like chilled ratatouille with a kick! You can set the terrine in individual moulds if you prefer, but it looks even better cut into slices.

1 medium aubergine (eggplant)
1 large red pepper, halved
1 large yellow pepper, halved
3 medium courgettes (zucchini),
*   trimmed*
6 sticks celery
2 sprigs rosemary
315ml (10 fl oz/1¼ cups) tomato
*   juice*

4 teaspoons powdered gelatine
dash of Worcestershire sauce
salt and pepper to taste
VODKA SAUCE:
grated rind of ½ lemon
4 tablespoons vodka
TO GARNISH:
pared lemon rind
rosemary sprigs

1 Preheat the oven to 190C (375F/Gas 5) and bake the aubergine (eggplant) and peppers for 20 minutes until slightly charred. Remove the core, seeds and skin from the peppers.

2 Cook courgettes (zucchini) in boiling water for 6 minutes. Remove from pan, refresh under cold water and drain. Blanch celery in the boiling water for 3 minutes; drain.

3 Add the rosemary to the tomato juice. Put 3 tablespoons of cold water in a cup, sprinkle on the gelatine and leave until spongy, then heat gently to dissolve. Stir into the tomato juice, with the Worcestershire sauce, salt and pepper.

4 Line a 625ml (1 pint) loaf tin or terrine with plastic wrap. Pour a thin layer of tomato juice over the base of the tin, discarding the rosemary. Chill until set.

5 Meanwhile, combine the vodka sauce ingredients in a bowl, cover and chill.

6 Cut the vegetables into strips, spoon into the prepared tin and pack down lightly. Carefully pour the remaining tomato juice over, then chill for at least 4 hours or preferably overnight, until firm.

7 Turn out the terrine, cut into slices and place on individual serving plates. Garnish with lemon rind and rosemary sprigs. Serve with the vodka sauce. *Serves 6.*

Salade Rapé

125g (4oz) carrot
125g (4oz) courgettes (zucchini),
  topped and tailed
125g (4oz) mooli or radish
125g (4oz) celeriac
125g (4oz) raw beetroot
3 tablespoons chopped parsley

NUT DRESSING:
4 tablespoons olive oil
2 tablespoons walnut or
  hazelnut oil
2 tablespoons lemon juice
1 clove garlic, crushed
salt and pepper to taste

1 Grate each of the vegetables in a food processor or mooli-grater; transfer to a bowl.
2 Whisk the dressing ingredients together in a bowl.
3 Just before serving, pour the dressing over the grated vegetables and toss lightly. Sprinkle with the parsley and serve with crusty bread. *Serves 4.*

Tricolore Salad

The simplest of all salads, and a perfect starter. Use as much fresh basil as you can afford. If you cannot find cocktail avocados, use a large, sliced avocado instead.

6 ripe tomatoes, sliced
250g (8oz) mozzarella cheese,
  sliced
12 cocktail avocados, peeled and
  halved
15-20 basil leaves

DRESSING:
6 tablespoons olive oil
2 tablespoons wine vinegar
1 teaspoon wine vinegar
1 teaspoon wholegrain mustard
pinch of sugar
salt and pepper to taste

1 Arrange the tomato and mozzarella slices in circles on individual plates. Pile the avocados in the middle and scatter basil leaves over the top.
2 Whisk the dressing ingredients together in a bowl and pour over the salad. Serve immediately. *Serves 4.*

Turkish Aubergines (Eggplants)

Also known as 'Imam Bayaldi', meaning 'the priest fainted'. As legend has it, the Imam collapsed when he tasted the delights of this dish! Be lavish with the olive oil – it makes all the difference.

*4 small or 2 large aubergines
  (eggplants)*
salt and pepper to taste
250ml (8 fl oz/1 cup) olive oil
2 large onions, thinly sliced
3 cloves garlic, crushed
*500g (1lb) tomatoes, skinned, or
  440g (14oz) can chopped
  tomatoes, drained*

*4 tablespoons chopped coriander
  leaves*
½ teaspoon ground cinnamon
1 teaspoon sugar
juice of ½ lemon
TO GARNISH:
*chopped coriander or parsley
  and extra sprigs*

1 Halve the aubergines (eggplants), scoop out the flesh, chop roughly and reserve, leaving 1cm (½ inch) thick shells. Sprinkle the shells with salt and place upside down on a board. Leave for 30 minutes to disgorge the bitter juices.
2 Heat 4 tablespoons olive oil in a saucepan, add the onions and cook gently for 10 minutes until soft but not browned. Add the garlic and cook for a further 2 minutes.
3 If using fresh tomatoes, halve them and squeeze out the seeds. Add the tomatoes to the onions with the coriander, cinnamon, chopped aubergine (eggplant), salt and pepper.
4 Preheat the oven to 150C (300F/Gas 2). Rinse the aubergines (eggplant) shells and pat dry with absorbent kitchen paper. Place, close together, in an ovenproof dish and spoon in the filling. Mix the remaining olive oil, sugar and lemon juice with 155ml (5 fl oz/⅔ cup) water and pour over and around the aubergines (eggplants). Cover and bake in the oven for 1 hour or until very soft. Cool, then chill for about 30 minutes.
5 Sprinkle with plenty of chopped coriander or parsley and garnish with extra sprigs to serve. *Serves 4.*

Crudités with Garlic Dip

I first tasted crudités on my very first French holiday in Provençe – truly one of discovery! My mother persuaded the housekeeper to make us the famous provençal dish of 'aioli'. She prepared the garlic mayonnaise with a pestle and mortar – in traditional style – and it 'sang' of garlic! Eaten with crisp vegetables, it tasted wonderful!

SELECTION OF THE FOLLOWING:
2 red or yellow peppers
12 radishes
12 baby carrots
½ cucumber
125g (4oz) small mange tout
  (snow peas) or sugar snap
  peas
12 baby corn
2 sticks celery
12 quail's eggs

AIOLI:
8 tablespoons good quality
  mayonnaise
2-3 cloves garlic, crushed
salt and pepper to taste
TO GARNISH:
herb sprigs

1 First prepare the aioli. In a bowl, mix the mayonnaise with the garlic and seasoning.
2 Halve and seed the peppers and cut into long wedges. Trim the radishes, leaving a little greenery on the ends. Peel and trim the carrots. Halve the cucumber lengthwise, scoop out the seeds and cut the flesh into sticks. Blanch the mange tout (snow peas) or sugar snaps, and baby corn in boiling water for 1 minute; refresh in cold water and drain. Trim celery and cut into sticks.
3 Place the quail's eggs in a saucepan containing cold water to cover and bring to the boil. Boil for 2 minutes, then plunge the eggs into cold water to cool. Partially peel the eggs.
4 Arrange the vegetables and eggs on a large platter or individual serving plates. Cover and chill until required. Garnish with herbs and serve with aioli. *Serves 4.*

Aubergine (Eggplant) Fritters

500g (1lb) thin aubergines
(eggplants)
salt and pepper to taste
155ml (5 fl oz/²⁄₃ cup) olive oil

3 tablespoons chopped mixed
herbs, eg. parsley, thyme,
oregano
2 × 220g (7oz) mozzarella
cheeses, thinly sliced

1 Cut the aubergines (eggplants) into 1cm (½ inch) thick slices. Place in a colander, sprinkle with salt and leave for 30 minutes to disgorge the bitter juices. Rinse under cold water and pat dry with absorbent kitchen paper. Spread over the base of a shallow dish.

2 Mix the olive oil with the herbs and drizzle over the aubergines (eggplants). Leave to stand for 15 minutes.

3 Preheat the grill. Arrange the aubergine (eggplant) slices on the grill pan and grill for 2-3 minutes until golden brown. Turn over, top each with a slice of mozzarella and grill until melted and bubbling. Season with pepper and serve piping hot, with crusty bread. *Serves 4.*

Tomato & Basil Bruschetta

These are commonly served all over Italy as an appetizer or snack with drinks.

2 very ripe large beef tomatoes
salt and pepper to taste
8 thick slices French bread

1 clove garlic, bruised
4 tablespoons olive oil
1 tablespoon shredded basil

1 Dip the tomatoes into boiling water for a count of ten. Lift out and plunge into cold water to stop further cooking. Peel the tomatoes, halve and remove the core and seeds. Roughly chop the flesh and mix with a little olive oil and seasoning.

2 Either toast or grill the bread until crisp and golden. Rub all over with the garlic and brush lightly with oil. Pile the tomato on top, sprinkle with basil and serve warm. *Serves 3-4.*

Garlic & Goat's Cheese Pizzette

This is one of my favourite starters, from one of my favourite restaurant menus in London. You *have* to use whole garlic cloves, or slices at least, for the full effect – just hold your breath the next day!

1 large red pepper
1 large yellow pepper
250g (8oz) packet pizza base mix
1 large beef tomato
8-12 cloves garlic, peeled

125g (4oz) fresh Welsh or
Somerset goat's cheese
salt and pepper to taste
olive oil for drizzling
2 tablespoons oregano or basil
leaves

1 Preheat the oven to 240C (475F/Gas 9); preheat the grill, too. Grill the peppers, turning occasionally, until blackened all over. Slip off the skins under cold water and remove the stalks and seeds. Cut into strips.

2 Make up the pizza dough following the manufacturer's instructions. Divide into 4 pieces and roll out each one thinly to a 13cm (5 inch) round on a lightly floured surface. Place on a baking sheet.

3 Dip the tomato into boiling water for a count of ten. Lift out and plunge into cold water to stop further cooking. Peel the tomato, halve and remove the core and seeds. Roughly chop the flesh.

4 Scatter the chopped tomato over the pizzette. Top with pepper strips, garlic cloves and crumbled goat's cheese. Add seasoning and drizzle with olive oil. Bake in the oven for 10-15 minutes, until bubbling. Slide the pizzette on to individual serving plates and scatter with herbs. Serve immediately. *Serves 4.*

Corn Pancakes with Guacamole

These little pancakes are similar to drop scones or Scotch pancakes – with the addition of creamed sweetcorn and cornmeal.

PANCAKES:
125g (4 oz/1 cup) plain flour
125g (4 oz/³⁄4 cup) maize or
  cornmeal
large pinch of salt
¹⁄2 teaspoon bicarbonate of soda
¹⁄2 teaspoon cream of tartar
¹⁄2 teaspoon chilli seasoning
1 small egg, beaten
315ml (10 fl oz/1¹⁄4 cups) milk
220g (7 oz) can creamed
  sweetcorn
butter for greasing

GUACAMOLE:
2 ripe avocados
1 small onion, grated
1 tablespoon lemon juice
1 tomato, skinned and seeded
2 tablespoons chopped coriander
  or parsley
salt and pepper to taste
TO SERVE:
155ml (5 fl oz/²⁄3 cup) thick sour
  cream
coriander or parsley sprigs

1 For the pancakes, sift together the flour, maize or cornmeal, salt, bicarbonate of soda, cream of tartar and chilli seasoning. Place in a blender or food processor with the egg and milk and blend until smooth. Transfer to a bowl and stir in the creamed corn. The mixture should be the consistency of thick cream; if too thick, add a little more milk. Leave to stand for 15 minutes.

2 Heat a griddle or heavy frying pan and grease with a little butter. Drop tablespoonfuls of the mixture on to the pan, placing them well apart. Cook for 1-2 minutes then carefully turn over and cook the other side. Wrap in foil and keep warm in a low oven. Repeat with the remaining batter to make about 20 pancakes.

3 Prepare the guacamole shortly before serving. Halve, stone and peel the avocados. Place in a bowl and mash roughly with a fork. Beat in the onion and lemon juice, then stir in the tomato, coriander or parsley, and seasoning.

4 To serve, spread pancakes with a little butter and top each with a mound of guacamole. Add a spoonful of sour cream and garnish with coriander or parsley. *Serves 4-6.*

Grilled Chicory with Feta

4 heads of chicory (witlof)
olive oil for basting
1 large ripe pear, cored and
  sliced

250g (8oz) feta cheese
1-2 teaspoons chopped thyme
freshly ground black pepper

1 Preheat the grill to high. Cut the chicory (witlof) in half lengthways and brush with oil. Place in the grill pan, cut side up, and grill (as near to the heat as possible) for 3-4 minutes, until just beginning to char and soften. Turn, baste with more oil and cook for a further 2-3 minutes.
2 Carefully turn again and top with pear slices. Brush with oil and grill for 1 minute. Sprinkle the feta and thyme on top and season with pepper. Grill until the cheese is brown and bubbling; the chicory should be very soft. Carefully transfer to warmed plates and serve. *Serves 4.*

Asparagus Mimosa

2 hard-boiled eggs, halved
90g (3oz) butter, softened
155ml (5 fl oz/²/₃ cup) thick sour
  cream
salt and pepper to taste

2 tablespoons chopped chervil or
  parsley
500g (1lb) asparagus
2 tablespoons lemon juice

1 Sieve the egg yolks and finely chop the whites. In a bowl, beat half of the yolks into the butter, then gradually beat in the sour cream. Season and stir in half of the herbs.
2 Trim off the woody ends from the asparagus, making sure they are all the same length. Bring a large, wide pan of water to the boil and add the lemon juice and a good pinch of salt. Add the asparagus and simmer for 10-15 minutes, depending on thickness, until tender; the asparagus should just yield when pierced with the tip of a sharp knife; drain.
3 Arrange on serving plates, sprinkle with remaining egg and herbs and serve with the dipping sauce. *Serves 4.*

Wild Mushroom Filo Tartlets

Tartlets as light as air filled with wild mushrooms if you have the courage to pick them! I have found wonderful chanterelles in a forest in my native Scotland – a magical find! A mixture of shitake, oyster and flat mushrooms would do just as well.

2-3 sheets frozen filo pastry,
    thawed
125g (4oz) butter, melted
1 clove garlic, crushed
2 shallots, finely chopped

375g (12oz) mixed mushrooms,
    wiped and roughly chopped
4 tablespoons white wine
salt and pepper to taste
herb sprigs to garnish

1 Preheat the oven to 200C (400F/Gas 6). Cut the filo pastry into twelve 10cm (4 inch) squares and brush liberally with melted butter. Lay a square in each of 4 individual 7.5cm (3 inch) flan tins. Cover each of these with another filo square, moving the tins a quarter-turn round. Repeat with remaining squares carefully frilling the edges and points, while retaining a good hollow in each centre. Bake in the oven for 8-10 minutes, until crisp and golden. Keep warm.

2 Heat the remaining butter in a frying pan, add the garlic and shallots and fry gently for 5 minutes until just turning golden. Add the mushrooms and white wine. Cook over a high heat for 2 minutes. Add seasoning.

3 Spoon the filling into the filo cases and garnish with herb sprigs. Serve immediately. *Serves 4.*

Stuffed Mushrooms

Sun-dried tomatoes with their concentrated caramelized tomato flavour make an excellent filling for stuffed mushrooms. They can be bought in Italian delicatessens – dried or preserved in oil; use the latter for this recipe. If you can't find them, use 2-3 fresh tomatoes instead, but the flavour won't be as good.

8 large cup mushrooms
6 tablespoons olive oil
2 rashers streaky bacon, rinds
  removed, chopped
4 shallots, finely chopped
8-12 sun-dried tomatoes in oil,
  drained and roughly chopped

2 tablespoons white wine
2 tablespoons balsamic or wine
  vinegar
salt and pepper to taste
2 tablespoons chopped parsley
parsley sprigs to garnish

1 Preheat the oven to 200C (400F/Gas 6). Remove the stalks from the mushrooms, roughly chop them and reserve.
2 Heat half of the oil in a frying pan, add the bacon and fry until golden. Add the shallots and cook over a gentle heat for 5 minutes until soft. Add the sun-dried tomatoes, wine, vinegar and chopped mushroom stalks. Cook for 2-3 minutes until reduced. Add seasoning.
3 Place the mushrooms, cup side up, on a baking sheet and spoon in the filling. Drizzle with the remaining olive oil and bake in the oven for 10 minutes. Transfer to individual serving plates and sprinkle with chopped parsley. Garnish with parsley sprigs and serve immediately. *Serves 4.*

Spaghetti Squash with Parmesan

Now is the time to discover one of the strangest vegetables ever – a real vegetable spaghetti! It's great fun to see people's faces as they pull out the golden strands!

2 small spaghetti squash
salt and pepper to taste
185g (6oz) butter
1 teaspoon paprika
1 tablespoon lemon juice

TO SERVE:
125g (4oz/1 cup) freshly grated
  Parmesan cheese
sprinkling of paprika
parsley sprigs

1 Cut the squash in half across the middle. Place in a large pan of boiling salted water and cook for 20 minutes.
2 Meanwhile, melt the butter in a small pan, add the paprika, lemon juice and pepper.
3 Drain the squash halves and remove any seeds. Remove a thin slice from the base of each one to enable them to stand upright. Place on warmed serving plates. Fluff up a little 'spaghetti' in the centre of each one with a fork, and pour in some paprika butter. Add a little of the Parmesan and sprinkle with paprika.
4 Garnish with parsley and hand the rest of the paprika butter and Parmesan separately. Let your guests pull out the strands of vegetable spaghetti dripping with butter – remember napkins! *Serves 4.*

Spaghettini with Tomato Sauce

The softer and redder the tomatoes are for this raw sauce, the better. Large beefsteak or marmande tomatoes are ideal, as are fresh ripe Italian plum tomatoes. The heat from the pasta releases the flavours of the raw tomatoes and sauce ingredients – to delicious effect.

250-375g (8-12oz) dried spaghettini or thin spaghetti
TOMATO SAUCE:
4 large ripe tomatoes
4 tablespoons shredded herbs, eg. basil, majoram, oregano, parsley, or a mixture of these

2 cloves garlic, finely chopped
125g (4oz/³/₄ cup) chopped black olives (optional)
155ml (5 fl oz/²/₃ cup) olive oil
salt and pepper to taste
TO GARNISH:
basil or parsley sprigs

1 To make the tomato sauce, plunge the tomatoes into a pan of boiling water and leave for 1 minute. Refresh under cold water and slip off the skins. Cut the tomatoes in half, squeeze out the seeds and chop the flesh into 1cm (½ inch) cubes. Place in a bowl with the herbs, garlic and olives if using. Add all but 2 tablespoons olive oil. Season and toss gently to mix. Allow the flavours to mingle for at least 30 minutes.

2 Drop the pasta into a large pan of boiling salted water, with the remaining oil added. Cook for 5-7 minutes, according to manufacturer's instructions, until *al dente* (cooked but firm to the bite).

3 Drain thoroughly and divide between warmed serving plates. Top with the tomato sauce and garnish with basil or parsley. Serve immediately. *Serves 4.*

Green Risotto

A pretty, but filling starter – follow with something very light! Arborio rice is the only rice that will give the correct creaminess to the risotto. Don't rush the pouring in of stock or you will have crunchy watery rice!

60g (2oz) butter
1 onion, finely chopped
625ml (1 pint/2½ cups) chicken
  or vegetable stock
375g (12oz) mixed broccoli
  florets and asparagus
280ml (9 fl oz/1 cup + 2tbsp)
  white wine

185g (6oz/1 cup) arborio or
  risotto rice
4-6 tablespoons chopped mixed
  herbs
4 tablespoons finely pared
  Parmesan cheese
parsley sprigs to garnish

1 Melt the butter in a saucepan, add the onion and cook gently for 5 minutes until soft, but not coloured.

2 Meanwhile, bring the stock to the boil in another pan. Add the green vegetables and simmer for 3 minutes; remove the vegetables with a slotted spoon and reserve. Pour the wine into the stock and keep simmering.

3 Add the rice to the onion and stir to coat. Add a ladleful of stock and stir gently over a low heat until absorbed. Repeat, ladleful at a time, until all the stock is absorbed and the rice is tender and creamy. Stir in the vegetables and herbs and heat through.

4 Transfer to warmed individual serving dishes and add the Parmesan. Serve immediately, garnished with parsley.
Serves 4.

Falafel with Mint Dressing

I first tasted falafel on my first trip to the States – it seemed so American to me – straight out of the movies! Made from chick peas, this Jewish speciality is either eaten as a starter or snack.

250g (8oz/1¼ cups) chick peas,
  soaked overnight
1 tablespoon olive oil
1 small egg, beaten
2 cloves garlic, crushed
pinch of chilli powder
½ teaspoon ground cumin
½ teaspoon ground coriander
salt and pepper to taste
8 water biscuits, crushed
olive oil for frying

SESAME MINT DRESSING:
2 tablespoons tahini (sesame
  seed paste)
2 tablespoons olive oil
juice of ½ lemon
3 tablespoons chopped mint
TO GARNISH:
mint sprigs
lemon wedges

1 Drain the chick peas and pat dry with absorbent kitchen paper. Place in a blender or food processor and process until finely ground. Add the oil, egg, garlic, spices and seasoning and work until smooth. Add half of the crushed water biscuits and blend to a smooth firm paste. If the mixture is too soft to roll into balls at this stage, add more crushed water biscuit until firm enough to handle.

2 For the sesame mint dressing, whisk all the ingredients together in a bowl, adding enough water to give a pouring consistency.

3 Divide the falafel mixture into about 20 equal pieces, roll into balls and flatten slightly. Heat a little olive oil in a frying pan and fry the falafel in batches until golden brown, about 3 minutes on each side; drain on absorbent kitchen paper and keep warm while cooking the remainder.

4 Serve immediately, garnished with mint and lemon wedges, and accompanied by the sesame mint dressing. *Serves 4.*

Roquefort & Hazelnut Soufflé

Don't be frightened by soufflés! They are easy to make and can be kept uncooked in the fridge until 15 minutes before serving – let your guests wait – the drama makes it all the more exciting!

45g (1½oz) butter
30g (1oz/¼ cup) plain flour
315ml (10 fl oz/1¼ cups) milk
155g (5oz) Roquefort or other
  blue cheese, crumbled
4 eggs, separated

125g (4oz/¾ cup) shelled
  hazelnuts, toasted and
  chopped
salt and pepper to taste
1 tablespoon chopped dill
dill sprigs to garnish

1 Preheat the oven to 190C (375F/Gas 5). Lightly grease 4 to 6 ramekins with butter.

2 Melt the butter in a small saucepan, add the flour and cook, stirring, for 1 minute. Remove from the heat and quickly pour in the milk, whisking constantly. Return to the heat and bring to the boil, whisking all the time to avoid lumps.

3 Stir in the Roquefort, egg yolks, three-quarters of the hazelnuts, salt, pepper and dill.

4 In a large bowl, whisk the egg whites with a pinch of salt until stiff. Stir a spoonful of the whisked egg whites into the cheese mixture, then carefully fold in the rest. Spoon into the ramekins and level the tops with a knife. Sprinkle with the remaining hazelnuts.

5 Bake in the oven for 15-20 minutes or until well risen and brown on top. Serve immediately, garnished with dill.
Serves 4-6.

Three Cheese Tartlets

The mozzarella in these savoury tartlets melts to give delicious pockets of molten cheese; the accompanying tomato salsa cuts through the richness.

250g (8oz) packet frozen
   shortcrust pastry, thawed
185g (6oz/¾ cup) fromage frais
2 eggs, beaten
60g (2oz) Parmesan cheese,
   freshly grated
salt and pepper to taste
grated nutmeg to taste
220g (7oz) mozzarella cheese

TOMATO SALSA:
2 large beef or plum tomatoes,
   skinned
8 basil leaves, shredded
2-3 teaspoons olive oil
TO GARNISH:
basil sprigs

1 Preheat the oven to 190C (375F/Gas 5). Roll out the pastry very thinly on a floured surface. Cut out four 15cm (6 inch) circles and use to line 7.5cm (3 inch) fluted flan tins. Trim off excess pastry. Line with greaseproof paper discs and baking beans and bake blind for 10 minutes. Remove paper and beans and bake for a further 5 minutes.

2 In a bowl, mix the fromage frais with the eggs and half of the Parmesan. Season with salt, pepper and nutmeg.

3 Cut the mozzarella into 1cm (½ inch) cubes and divide equally between the pastry cases. Pour in the egg and cheese mixture and sprinkle with the remaining Parmesan. Bake for 15-20 minutes until firm and golden brown.

4 Meanwhile, make the tomato salsa. Halve the tomatoes and discard seeds. Roughly chop the flesh and mix with the basil, olive oil, salt and pepper.

5 Place each tartlet on a warmed serving plate and add a generous spoonful of tomato salsa. Garnish with basil and serve immediately. *Serves 4.*

NOTE: These tartlets must be freshly made or you won't have lovely pockets of melted cheese in the middle!

Oriental Omelette Salad

2 large eggs
salt
2 tablespoons sunflower oil
1 teaspoon sesame oil
1cm (½ inch) piece fresh root
  (green) ginger, finely chopped

1 clove garlic, finely chopped
250g (8oz) spinach, rinsed and
  stalks removed
250g (8oz) peeled prawns
4 spring onions (green shallots),
  sliced

1 Beat the eggs with a little salt and preheat a small non-stick frying pan. Pour 3 tablespoons egg into the pan and swirl round to thinly cover the bottom. Cook until set, then remove, roll up and slice into thin rounds; set aside. Repeat with remaining egg.
2 Heat the oils in a frying pan and add the ginger and garlic. Quickly add all the remaining ingredients and toss over moderate heat until the spinach is just wilted.
3 Spoon on to warmed serving plates and top with the omelette rolls. Serve immediately. *Serves 4.*

Quail's Eggs in Asparagus Nest

12 fresh quail's eggs
500g (1lb) sprue asparagus
salt and pepper to taste

1 slice ham, cut into strips
125g (4oz) unsalted butter,
  melted

1 Place the quail's eggs in a shallow pan and cover with cold water. Bring to the boil and boil for 1 minute. Drain, cover with cold water and partially peel when cool enough to handle.
2 Trim asparagus, cut into 5cm (2 inch) lengths and cook in boiling salted water for 2 minutes; drain.
3 Toss asparagus with ham and arrange in 'nests' on warmed individual plates. Place 3 quail's eggs in each nest. Top with melted butter and seasoning to serve. *Serves 4.*

Scrambled Egg Brioche

When cooking for a very grand lady, I once served scrambled eggs in the empty warmed pastry case of a *foie gras en croûte* for breakfast – outrageous but wonderful! This is a humble version.

4 small brioches
60g (2oz) butter, melted
4 eggs, beaten
2 tablespoons thick sour cream
salt and pepper to taste

60g (2oz) pot salmon roe, or
   lumpfish roe
2 tablespoons snipped chives
few chives to garnish

1 Preheat the oven to 140C (275F/Gas 1). Cut the tops off the brioches and reserve. Using a sharp knife, hollow out the bases, leaving a 1cm (½ inch) shell; discard the crumbs. Brush the insides with a little of the melted butter and warm in the oven for 2-3 minutes.

2 Meanwhile, make the scrambled eggs. Pour the remaining butter into a small non-stick pan. Beat the eggs, sour cream, salt and pepper together and pour into the pan. Cook over a gentle heat for 1-2 minutes, stirring all the time, until thickened and still creamy; do not overcook or you will have watery separated eggs. Stir in all but 4 teaspoons of the salmon roe and half of the snipped chives.

3 Place the brioches on warmed serving plates. Spoon the scrambled eggs into the brioches and top each with a spoonful of roe and a sprinkling of chives. Replace the lids, if desired. Lay a couple of chives across each plate and serve immediately. *Serves 4.*

Gnocchi with Walnut Pesto

These little dumplings are light and airy if handled carefully – a perfect foil for the rich nutty walnut sauce.

250g (8oz) ricotta or curd cheese
60g (2oz) butter, softened
125g (4oz) Parmesan cheese,
  freshly grated
1 egg, size 2, beaten
3 tablespoons (9tsp) plain flour
salt and pepper to taste
grated nutmeg to taste

WALNUT PESTO:
1 clove garlic, crushed
60g (2oz/²⁄₃ cup) walnut halves
45g (1¹⁄₂ oz) basil leaves, stalks
  removed
3 tablespoons freshly grated
  thinly pared Parmesan cheese
155ml (5 fl oz/²⁄₃ cup) olive oil
TO SERVE:
basil leaves to garnish
thinly pared Parmesan cheese

1 Sieve the ricotta or curd cheese into a bowl and add the butter, Parmesan, egg and flour. Beat until smooth, seasoning with salt, pepper and nutmeg. Cover and chill in the refrigerator for at least 1 hour or overnight.

2 Meanwhile, make the walnut pesto. Place the garlic, walnuts, basil leaves, cheese and salt in a blender or food processor and blend until smooth. With the machine still running, gradually pour in the olive oil; the pesto will thicken as the oil is absorbed.

3 Bring a large pan of salted water to the boil. Lower the heat and add heaped teaspoonfuls of gnocchi mixture to the simmering water. Poach gently for 3-4 minutes or until they rise to the surface. Remove with a slotted spoon and drain.

4 Pile the gnocchi on to warmed individual plates and top each serving with a generous dollop of pesto. Garnish with basil and serve immediately, with extra Parmesan handed separately. *Serves 4.*

Shellfish Platter

It would be hard to beat those found in France, but a simple version – using as varied a selection of fresh seafood as possible – is a lovely way to start a meal. Choose a selection of raw and cooked seafood – don't even attempt to use seafood preserved in vinegar – sacrilege!

8 live mussels
8 live oysters
4 live cooked lobster tails
4 crab claws
250g (8oz) cooked baby clams or
  winkles
8 cooked king prawns

250g (8oz) cooked whole
  shrimps (optional)
TO SERVE:
crushed ice or crystal salt
lemon and lime wedges
seaweed to garnish

1 Scrub the mussels, removing the beards, and rinse well. Leave to soak in a bowl of cold water for 30 minutes, then tap each mussel sharply; discard any that do not close straight away. Remove the empty half-shells.

2 To prepare each oyster, hold in a clean cloth or glove, deep-side in the palm of your hand. Insert an oyster knife at the hinged end, lever and twist the knife between the hinge until it separates. Sever the muscle from the flat top shell, discarding top shell. Loosen the meat from the inside shell and turn meat over, taking care not to spill any juice.

3 Line individual serving plates with a layer of crushed ice or salt crystals. Arrange all the seafood on top and garnish with citrus wedges and seaweed. Serve immediately, with brown bread and butter. *Serves 4.*

NOTE: If preferred, cook the mussels in a little wine until the shells open, discarding any that do not, and serve cooked.

If fresh seafood is difficult to find, try a selection of smoked fish and shellfish, such as smoked salmon and turbot, mussels and scallops.

Prawns in 'Seaweed' Nests

Chinese crispy 'seaweed' is not seaweed at all but spring greens! This recipe is authentic, easy to make and an excellent starter.

12 large (king) prawns
melted butter for brushing
TO GARNISH:
toasted almonds or pine nuts

SEAWEED:
375g (12oz) spring greens or
    cabbage leaves
oil for frying
1 teaspoon salt
1 teaspoon caster sugar

1 First, prepare the 'seaweed'. Remove the thick stalks from the spring greens or cabbage. Roll each leaf tightly from the bottom and slice as finely as possible, using a very sharp knife.

2 Pour oil into a large saucepan to a depth of 5cm (2 inches). Heat the oil to 200C (400F) or until a cube of bread browns in 30 seconds. Add half of the spring greens and fry for about 1 minute until crisp but still retaining their colour. Immediately remove and drain on absorbent kitchen paper. Fry the remaining spring greens or cabbage in the same way. Drain and sprinkle with the salt and sugar.

3 Preheat the grill to high. Pull the legs and head off the prawns. With a sharp knife, make a shallow incision along the back of each prawn to expose the black intestinal vein, then remove it. Rinse prawns under cold water and pat dry.

4 Brush each prawn with melted butter and place on the grill rack. Grill for about 2 minutes on each side or until pink and firm.

5 Make a 'nest' of 'seaweed' on each of 4 individual serving plates. Place 3 prawns in the centre of each nest and scatter with toasted nuts. Pour over any remaining melted butter, if desired. Serve immediately. *Serves 4.*

Coconut Crusted Prawns

Serve these spicy prawns with a cucumber raita – seasoned yogurt mixed with diced cucumber – and cherry tomatoes.

125g (4oz/1⅓ cups) desiccated
  coconut
2 cloves garlic, crushed
1 small green chilli, seeded
½ teaspoon turmeric
1 teaspoon ground cumin

1 teaspoon ground coriander
salt and pepper to taste
grated rind and juice of 1 large
  lime
12 raw jumbo prawns, peeled
125g (4oz) butter, melted

1 Preheat the grill to medium and line grill pan with foil. Put coconut, garlic, chilli, spices, seasoning and lime rind in a blender or food processor with half of the lime juice. Blend to a paste, adding more lime juice if needed.
2 Press paste all over prawns, place on grill pan and drizzle with melted butter. Grill for 2-3 minutes on each side until golden brown, basting occasionally with melted butter. Serve hot, with raita. *Serves 4.*

Oysters with Pumpernickel

24 live oysters
SHALLOT VINEGAR:
2 shallots, finely chopped
6 tablespoons wine vinegar

TO SERVE:
sea salt
lemon wedges
4 slices pumpernickel

1 To prepare each oyster, hold in a clean cloth or glove, deep-side in the palm of your hand. Insert oyster knife at hinge end, lever and twist knife between hinge until it separates. Sever muscle from flat top shell, discarding top shell. Loosen meat from inside shell and turn meat over, taking care not to spill any juice. Arrange on serving plates lined with salt.
2 Mix the shallots with the vinegar and pour a little shallot vinegar over each oyster. Serve with lemon wedges and pumpernickel. *Serves 4.*

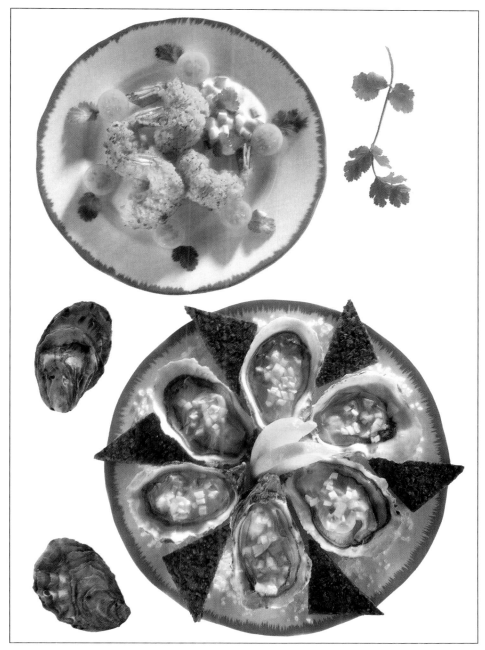

Blinis

A Russian favourite of mine: yeasty pancakes made with buckwheat and plain flour; topped with thick sour cream and caviare or lumpfish roe. Chopped hard-boiled egg and onion are also popular accompaniments. I like to serve tiny blinis with drinks as canapés.

125g (4oz/1 cup) buckwheat or wholemeal flour
1 tablespoon easy-blend yeast
1 teaspoon sugar
375ml (12 fl oz/1½ cups) warm milk
125g (4oz/1 cup) plain flour
pinch of salt
2 eggs
1 tablespoon melted butter

oil or lard for frying
butter for spreading
TOPPINGS:
thick sour cream
lumpfish roe or caviare
smoked salmon
pickled herring
chopped hard-boiled egg
chopped onion

1 In a large bowl, mix the buckwheat or wholemeal flour with the easy-blend yeast and sugar. Gradually beat in half of the warm milk.

2 Sift the plain flour and salt into another bowl. Make a well in the centre and add 1 whole egg, plus 1 yolk. Add the remaining milk and melted butter. Beat well to form a smooth batter, then beat into the yeast mixture. Cover the bowl with plastic wrap and leave to rise in a warm place for 1-2 hours.

3 Whisk the reserved egg white and fold into the batter. Preheat a heavy pan or griddle and grease with oil or lard. Drop tablespoons of the batter on to the griddle or pan, spacing them well apart. Turn over when bubbles appear on the surface and cook until just turning brown.

4 Spread immediately with a little butter, wrap in foil and keep warm in a preheated cool oven. Put the toppings into serving bowls and allow everyone to add their choice to the blinis. *Serves 4.*

Crab Ravioli with Chive Sauce

A cheat's method of making 'ravioli' – but very successful. If preferred, you can use lobster tails or prawns instead of crab. If time, try making your own pasta – rolling it out very thinly.

4 sheets fresh lasagne
CRAB FILLING:
250g (8oz) fresh mixed crab
  meat (or frozen and thawed)
4 tablespoon double (thick)
  cream
pinch of ground ginger
pinch of ground mace
salt and pepper to taste

CHIVE BUTTER SAUCE:
1 shallot, finely chopped
3 tablespoons (9 tsp) white wine
  vinegar
250g (8oz) unsalted butter,
  chilled and cubed
squeeze of lemon juice
2 tablespoons chopped chives
TO GARNISH:
few chives

1 To make the crab filling, in a small pan, mix together the crab, cream, spices and seasoning. Warm through over a low heat, then keep warm.

2 For the chive butter sauce, put the shallot and vinegar in a small pan with 3 tablespoons water. Boil until reduced to 2 tablespoons. Over a low heat, gradually whisk in the butter, a piece at a time, until creamy and amalgamated; this process shouldn't take too long. Do not allow to boil or the sauce will separate. Season with salt and pepper and stir in the lemon juice and chives. Keep warm in a bowl, placed over a pan of hot water.

3 Cut each lasagne sheet in half to give 8 large squares. Cook in plenty of boiling salted water, according to manufacturer's instructions, until *al dente* (cooked but still firm to the bite). Drain and toss in a little of the sauce.

4 Place a pasta square on each of 4 warmed serving plates. Divide the crab filling between them and top with the remaining pasta squares. Spoon a little chive butter sauce over the pasta and garnish with chives. Serve immediately. *Serves 4.*

Mouclade

This mussel stew from Brittany makes a delicious change from *moules marinière*. It is quite rich, so serve something light to follow.

2.25 litres (4 pints/10 cups) live
   mussels
155ml (5 fl oz/²/₃ cup) dry white
   wine
2 shallots, finely chopped
30g (1oz) butter
2 cloves garlic, crushed
2 teaspoons potato flour or
   cornflour

315ml (10 fl oz/1¼ cups) double
   (thick) cream
pinch of saffron threads
salt and pepper to taste
juice of ½ lemon
   (approximately)
1 egg yolk
1 tablespoon chopped parsley
parsley sprigs to garnish

1 Scrub the mussels, removing the beards, and rinse well. Leave to soak in a bowl of cold water for 30 minutes, then tap each mussel sharply; discard any that do not close straight away.

2 Drain the mussels and place in a large saucepan. Add the wine and shallots, cover and cook over a high heat, shaking the pan frequently, for 5-10 minutes until the mussels open; discard any that remain closed at this stage.

3 Drain the mussels, reserving the liquid. Remove all empty half shells and keep the mussels warm. Boil the reserved liquid rapidly until reduced by half.

4 Melt the butter in a saucepan, add the garlic and cook until golden. Add the flour, then gradually stir in the reserved liquid. Add the cream, saffron and seasoning and simmer until slightly thickened. Add lemon juice to taste and stir in the egg yolk.

5 Divide the mussels between individual serving bowls and pour the sauce over them. Sprinkle with parsley and garnish with extra sprigs. Serve immediately, with lots of crusty bread. *Serves 4.*

Warm Scallop & Bacon Salad

Otherwise known as a 'salade tiede' or warm salad, this is always popular. Use any combination of mixed bitter salad leaves. Make sure everyone has a napkin in case the dressing splashes!

6 fresh scallops
3 tablespoons olive oil
125g (4oz) pancetta or streaky
* bacon, derinded and sliced*
½ small frisée (curly endive)
handful of lamb's lettuce (corn
* salad)*
few radicchio leaves and/or oak
* leaf lettuce*
TO GARNISH:
parsley sprigs

DRESSING:
6 tablespoons olive oil
2 tablespoons sherry or wine
* vinegar*
2 cloves garlic, finely chopped
1 teaspoon Dijon mustard
salt and pepper to taste
2 tablespoons double (thick)
* cream (optional)*

1 To make the dressing, whisk together the oil, vinegar, garlic, mustard and seasoning in a small saucepan, until thickened. Heat gently and keep warm.

2 Remove the tough muscle opposite the coral on each scallop. Separate the coral and cut the scallops in half horizontally. Lightly score each scallop disc in a lattice pattern with a sharp knife.

3 Heat the oil in a frying pan, add the bacon and fry over a high heat until brown and crisp. Add the scallops, including the coral, and stir-fry for 2-3 minutes until just opaque.

4 Arrange the salad leaves on individual serving plates. Top with the bacon and scallop mixture. Whisk the cream into the warm dressing, pour over the salad and serve immediately, garnished with parsley. *Serves 4.*

Grilled Ceviche

This starter was a revelation to me when I first tasted it in a fashionable London restaurant. It is so simple, and the initial grilling gives the fish a fabulous smoky flavour.

185g (6oz) salmon fillet,
*   skinned and boned*
185g (6oz) fresh tuna or
*   monkfish, skinned and boned*
olive oil for brushing
MARINADE:
thinly pared rind and juice of
*   1 lime*

4 tablespoons olive oil
1 small red chilli, seeded
salt and pepper to taste
TO SERVE:
1 small green pepper, halved,
*   seeded and diced*
1 tablespoon chopped coriander
coriander sprigs to garnish

1 Make sure all bones have been removed from the fish. Brush a heavy frying pan with a little olive oil and place over a high heat until smoking. Quickly add the fish to the pan and cook for 20 seconds on one side. Turn over and cook on the other side for 20 seconds only; the pan must be very hot to seal the fish on the outside without cooking the inside. Remove the fish from the pan and cool completely.

2 To prepare the marinade, in a shallow dish, mix together the lime rind and juice and the olive oil. Thinly slice the chilli into rings and add to the dish.

3 Cut the fish into thin strips or chunks, add to the marinade and toss carefully to mix. Cover and leave to marinate in the refrigerator for 1 hour.

4 Lift the fish out of the marinade and arrange on individual serving plates. Season the marinade and add the coriander. Scatter the green pepper over the fish and spoon the marinade over the ceviche to serve. *Serves 4.*

NOTE: Alternatively the fish can be sealed quickly on a very hot barbecue.

Herring & Beetroot Salad

8 marinated herring fillets,
    drained
250g (8oz) freshly cooked
    beetroot, skinned and diced
250g (8oz) cooked new potatoes,
    halved

handful of mixed salad leaves,
    eg. frisée (curly endive),
    radicchio
155ml (5 fl oz/²/₃ cup) thick sour
    cream
2 tablespoons chopped chives

1 Arrange the herring fillets on individual plates with the beetroot, potatoes and salad leaves. Add a generous spoonful of sour cream and sprinkle with chopped chives.

2 Serve with dark rye bread. *Serves 4.*

Marinated Anchovy Salad

Marinated anchovies are soft, silvery and slightly piquant; they bear no resemblance to canned anchovies in oil. They are available in jars from delicatessens, but if you cannot find them, use fine strips of marinated herring instead.

2 red peppers, halved
2 yellow peppers, halved
185g (6oz) marinated anchovies,
    drained
TO SERVE:
2 tablespoons chopped parsley
2 hard-boiled eggs

DRESSING:
155ml (5 fl oz/²/₃ cup) mixed
    olive and sunflower oil
1 tablespoon wine or cider
    vinegar
salt and pepper to taste

1 Preheat the grill to high and grill the peppers until blackening all over. Slip off the skins under cold water and remove the stalks and seeds. Cut into wide strips.

2 Arrange the pepper strips and anchovies on individual serving plates. Whisk the ingredients for the dressing together and spoon over the salad.

3 Chop the egg whites and sieve the yolks. Scatter over the salad and sprinkle liberally with parsley. Serve immediately. *Serves 4.*

Tartare of Salmon & Cucumber

I prefer this to gravad lax. It tastes much cleaner and looks most attractive with its green and pink marbling.

500g (1lb) boned salmon,
  skinned
finely grated rind and juice of 1
  lime
1 tablespoon sugar
salt and pepper to taste
½ cucumber (unpeeled), finely
  grated

1 teaspoon tarragon or herb
  mustard
1-2 tablespoons thick sour
  cream
1 tablespoon chopped dill
TO GARNISH:
herb sprigs
lime slices

1 Oil four 125ml (4 fl oz/½ cup) ramekins or individual moulds. Check that all bones have been removed from the salmon; remove any odd ones with tweezers and place the salmon in a shallow dish.

2 In a small bowl, mix the lime rind and juice with the sugar and 1 tablespoon salt; rub into the salmon. Cover and leave to marinate in the refrigerator for at least 4 hours, turning once.

3 Sprinkle the cucumber with 1 tablespoon salt, toss gently and transfer to a colander. Leave to drain for 30 minutes.

4 Lift the salmon out of the marinade and pat dry. Cut into tiny dice and place in a bowl with the mustard, sour cream, chopped dill and seasoning. Rinse the cucumber and pat dry. Add to the salmon and mix well. Pack into the prepared moulds, cover and chill for at least 1 hour.

5 Turn out on to small plates and decorate with herb sprigs and lime slices. Serve with black rye bread or pumpernickel. *Serves 4.*

Smoked Salmon Bundles

This simple starter can be rustled up very quickly. Filo pastry freezes well, so it's always worth keeping a packet in the freezer.

3 sheets filo pastry, thawed if frozen
melted butter for brushing
FILLING:
185g (6oz) smoked salmon, diced
375g (12oz) ricotta or curd cheese
2 tablespoons chopped chives or dill
pinch of ground nutmeg
salt and pepper to taste

DILL BUTTER SAUCE:
1 shallot, finely chopped
3 tablespoons (9 tsp) white wine vinegar
3 tablespoons water
250g (8oz) unsalted butter, chilled and cubed
squeeze of lemon juice
2 tablespoons chopped dill or fennel
TO GARNISH:
dill or fennel sprigs

1 Preheat the oven to 200C (400F/Gas 6). To make the filling, in a bowl mix together the salmon, ricotta or curd cheese, chives or dill, nutmeg and seasoning, until smooth.

2 Cut the filo pastry into twelve to sixteen 10cm (4 inch) squares. Brush with melted butter and place a spoonful of salmon filling in the middle of each square. Draw the pastry up around the filling, pinching to form a money-bag shape. Spread the frilly tops decoratively.

3 Place on a greased baking sheet and brush with melted butter. Bake in the oven for 10-15 minutes until golden brown.

4 Meanwhile make the dill butter sauce. Put the shallot, vinegar and water in a small pan. Bring to the boil and boil steadily until reduced to 2 tablespoons. Over a low heat, gradually whisk in the butter, a piece at a time, until creamy and amalgamated; this process shouldn't take too long. Do not allow to boil or the sauce will separate. Stir in the dill or fennel and seasoning.

5 Arrange the smoked salmon bundles on individual serving plates and tie a herb sprig around each one. Spoon a little sauce around them and serve immediately. *Serves 4.*

Striped Fish Terrine

The secret of making a light fish mousseline is to chill all the ingredients thoroughly beforehand.

375g (12oz) boned salmon,
  skinned
1 egg white
155ml (5 fl oz/²⁄₃ cup) double
  (thick) cream
lemon juice to taste
salt and pepper to taste
375g (12oz) sole fillets, skinned

2 tablespoons chopped dill
1 tablespoon chopped tarragon
  or parsley
butter for greasing
TO FINISH:
mustard and cress
crème fraîche

1 Cut the salmon into 2.5cm (1 inch) pieces, place in a blender or food processor and purée until smooth. Add the egg white and blend again until evenly mixed. Place in the refrigerator and chill for at least 30 minutes.

2 Return to the blender or food processor and add the cream, lemon juice and seasoning. Blend until smooth. Chill for 30 minutes.

3 Cut the sole fillets into long strips and roll in the chopped herbs until well coated.

4 Preheat the oven to 180C (350F/Gas 4). Grease a 625ml (20 fl oz/2½ cup) loaf tin or terrine with butter. Spoon one third of the salmon mixture into the tin and spread evenly. Lay the herbed sole strips on top, leaving a border at each side. Carefully spoon the remaining salmon mixture over the sole. Spread evenly and level the surface.

5 Cover with buttered foil and place in a roasting tin, containing enough hot water to come half-way up the sides of the terrine. Bake in the oven for 35 minutes or until a skewer inserted into the centre comes out clean.

6 Lift the terrine out of the roasting tin and leave until cold. Remove the foil, cover with oiled greaseproof paper and weight down. Chill for at least 4 hours before carefully turning out. Cut into slices, garnish with mustard and cress and serve with crème fraîche. *Serves 4-6.*

Chicken Liver Mousse

Rich and creamy, this is my version of an old favourite. Do try to use Marsala, a soft and pungent fortified wine from Sicily – it imparts a warm, almost nutty flavour.

375g (12oz) chicken livers
salt and pepper to taste
1 tablespoon Marsala or brandy
1 tablespoon olive oil
250g (8oz) butter, softened

125ml (4 fl oz/½ cup) double
* (thick) or whipping cream*
125ml (4 fl oz/½ cup) clarified
* butter*
8 sage leaves
salad leaves to garnish

1 Pick over the chicken livers; cut out and discard any bitter 'green' bits and any fatty 'strings'. Rinse under cold water and pat dry with absorbent kitchen paper.

2 Sprinkle the livers with a little salt and pepper. Place in a shallow dish with the Marsala or brandy and olive oil. Cover and leave to marinate in a cool place for 1-2 hours, if time.

3 Place a non-stick frying pan over a low heat and add the livers with the marinade. Cook very gently for 10-12 minutes or until they are firm but still pink in the middle when pierced with a sharp knife; the livers should not brown. Allow to cool slightly.

4 Purée the livers in a blender or food processor, gradually adding the butter and working until smooth. Add the cream and blend for 2-3 seconds. Check the seasoning.

5 Spoon the mousse into individual pots, smooth the surface and cover each with a thin layer of clarified butter and a couple of sage leaves. Allow to set. Serve garnished with salad leaves and accompanied by hot toast or crisp melba toast. *Serves 4.*

TO CLARIFY BUTTER: Cut into cubes and melt slowly in a heavy saucepan over a low heat; do not allow to boil. Carefully spoon off the clear butter, leaving the milky sediment behind. Store the clarified butter in a jar in the refrigerator for up to 2 weeks.

Jewelled Venison Salad

Smoked venison is becoming more widely available in delicatessens and by post from Scotland. It has a wonderful reddish brown colour and tastes like gamey smoked ham.

2 small oranges
1 pomegranate
12-16 slices smoked venison (or
    smoked chicken)

DRESSING:
2 tablespoons orange juice
1 tablespoon olive oil
pinch of ground cumin
salt and pepper to taste

1 Peel and segment the oranges, discarding all pith and rind; catch any juice in a bowl and reserve for the dressing.
2 Halve the pomegranate, scoop out the seeds and reserve.
3 Arrange the venison, orange segments and pomegranate seeds on individual serving plates. Whisk the dressing ingredients together and spoon over the salad. *Serves 4.*

Bresaola with Pear & Gorgonzola

I'm crazy about Italian food! This salad of air-dried beef, luscious pears and creamy gorgonzola is totally indulgent.

185-250g (6-8oz) gorgonzola
4-8 slices bresaola
2 ripe pears

olive oil for drizzling
freshly ground black pepper
black olives to garnish

1 Crumble the gorgonzola and divide equally between the slices of bresaola. Roll up or fold over and set aside.
2 Halve and core the pears. Slice finely and arrange on individual serving plates with the bresaola. Drizzle with olive oil and sprinkle with pepper. Garnish with olives to serve. *Serves 4.*

Chicken & Two Pepper Terrine

The combination of roasted red and yellow peppers, tarragon and chicken make this a stunning starter that is very simple to prepare.

375g (12oz) skinned boneless
  chicken breast, trimmed
2 egg whites, lightly beaten
375ml (12 fl oz/1½ cups) double
  (thick) or whipping cream
2 tablespoons (6 tsp) chopped
  tarragon

salt and pepper to taste
2 red peppers
2 yellow peppers
TO SERVE:
salad leaves
nut oil for dressing, eg. walnut
  or hazelnut oil

1 Preheat the grill. Mince the chicken finely in a food processor. With the machine running, quickly add the egg whites and cream and process for a few seconds only; do not over-process or the mixture will curdle. Turn into a bowl and beat in the tarragon and seasoning. Cover and chill in the refrigerator for 20 minutes.

2 Meanwhile, grill the peppers, turning frequently, until charred all over. Slip off the skins under cold running water and remove the stalks and seeds. Cut the peppers into wide strips.

3 Preheat the oven to 150C (300F/Gas 2). Spread three-quarters of the chicken mixture evenly over the base and sides of a 500g (1lb) non-stick loaf tin. Arrange the yellow pepper in the centre, packing it down firmly. Top with the red pepper and cover with the remaining chicken mixture.

4 Cover the tin with buttered foil and place in a bain-marie, or roasting tin containing enough water to come halfway up the side of the loaf tin. Bake in the oven for 25 minutes. Allow to cool with a weight on top. Refrigerate when cold.

5 To serve, turn out and cut into slices. Arrange on serving plates, with salad leaves tossed in nut oil. *Serves 4-6.*

Prosciutto with Exotic Fruits

A most attractive and refreshing starter. (Illustrated on page 1).

8 lychees
1 mango
1 paw paw (papaya)
1 sharon fruit

2 kiwi fruit
8 slices prosciutto (Parma ham)
freshly ground black pepper

1 Partially peel the lychees. Peel and slice the mango, discarding the stone. Peel and halve the pawpaw, scoop out the black seeds and cut the flesh into cubes. Slice the sharon fruit into rounds. Peel and slice the kiwi fruit.
2 Arrange the prosciutto and fruits on individual plates. Sprinkle with black pepper. *Serves 4.*

Duck Breast on Potato Pancakes

1 large potato, about 375g
    (12oz), peeled
4 tablespoons oil
2 boned duck breasts
3 tablespoons raspberry vinegar

1 teaspoon chopped thyme
salt and pepper to taste
thyme sprigs and roasted garlic
    cloves to garnish

1 Finely grate potato and squeeze out all moisture. Heat 1 tablespoon oil in a small heavy frying pan. Add a quarter of the potato and press firmly with a fish slice to fuse the mixture together. Cook for 2 minutes on each side, or until golden brown. Drain on absorbent kitchen paper and keep warm. Repeat to make 3 more potato pancakes.
2 Score a criss-cross pattern on the duck breast skin. Heat a frying pan and place duck in pan, skin-side down. Fry slowly for about 8 minutes until most of the fat has run out and the skin is golden. Turn over and cook for a further 2 minutes. Remove from the pan and slice thickly.
3 Pour off fat from pan, then add the vinegar and thyme. Bring to the boil and pour over the duck. Serve immediately, garnished with thyme and garlic. *Serves 4.*

Chicken & Water Chestnut Kebabs

These little kebabs are very quick to make. Pancetta is a type of Italian streaky bacon and can be bought in a piece to cut into any size. Alternatively, use ordinary streaky bacon and form into little rolls before skewering.

3 large skinned boneless chicken breasts
2 tablespoons light soy sauce
2cm (¾ inch) piece fresh root (green) ginger, sliced
1 clove garlic, crushed

250g (8oz) pancetta or streaky bacon
300g (10oz) can water chestnuts (about 24 chestnuts), drained
salad leaves to garnish

1 Preheat the grill to high. Cut the chicken into 2cm (¾ inch) cubes and place in a shallow dish. Add the soy sauce, ginger and garlic and toss well. Cover and leave to marinate in a cool place for at least 15 minutes.

2 Remove rind from the pancetta or bacon and cut into forty-eight 2cm (¾ inch) squares, 5mm (¼ inch) thick.

3 Drain the chicken, reserving the marinade. Thread the chicken, pancetta and chestnuts alternately on to 12 small bamboo skewers.

4 Cook under the preheated grill for about 4 minutes per side or until crisp and tender, basting frequently with the marinade. Serve immediately, on a bed of salad leaves. *Serves 6.*

NOTE: To prevent burning, pre-soak the bamboo skewers in cold water before use.

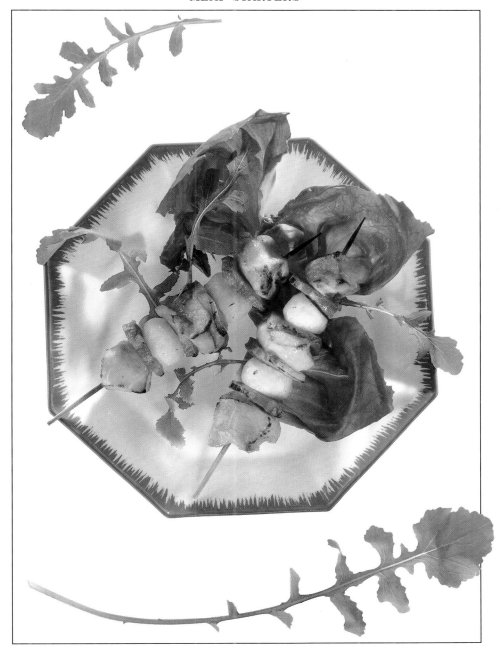

Chicken Livers with Polenta

Polenta is made from cornmeal and usually takes ages to cook, but 5-minute versions can be found in Italian delicatessens. So can excellent balsamic vinegar, with its rich sweet sour taste – acquired during ageing in wooden barrels.

1 packet quick-cook polenta mix
250g (8oz) chicken livers
2 tablespoons olive oil
2 tablespoons balsamic or sherry
  vinegar

1 tablespoon chopped sage
salt and pepper to taste
30g (1oz) butter, melted
sage sprigs to garnish

1 Make up the polenta according to packet directions. Pour into a deep bowl and leave in a cool place for 30 minutes to set.

2 Pick over the chicken livers; cut out and discard any bitter 'green' bits and any fatty 'strings'. Rinse under cold water and pat dry with absorbent kitchen paper.

3 Heat the oil in a non-stick frying pan until hot but not smoking. Add the chicken livers and stir-fry over high heat for about 2 minutes until well browned. Transfer to a plate, using a slotted spoon, and set aside.

4 Preheat the grill to high. Add the vinegar to the juices in the pan and allow to bubble over a gentle heat for 1 minute, scraping up any sediment from the bottom of the pan. Drain the chicken livers, add to the pan and stir-fry for a further 4-5 minutes until firm and just pink inside. Stir in the sage and seasoning. Keep warm.

5 Meanwhile, turn out the polenta and cut into 8 pieces. Brush with melted butter and grill for 1 minute on each side or until browned. Place on individual plates and top with the livers. Garnish with sage and serve immediately. *Serves 4.*

VARIATION: Use thickly sliced French bread in place of the polenta slices.

Pork Satay with Cucumber Salad

A Malaysian friend showed me how to make this crunchy cucumber salad when we were preparing the food for an Oriental/English wedding. It goes perfectly with pork satay.

SATAY:
500g (1lb) pork fillet
1 tablespoon dark soy sauce
2 teaspoons light soy sauce
2 tablespoons crunchy peanut
   butter
1cm (½ inch) piece fresh root
   (green) ginger, finely chopped
TO GARNISH:
spring onion (shallot) brushes

CUCUMBER SALAD:
½ cucumber, peeled
salt
1 tablespoon caster sugar
60ml (2 fl oz/¼ cup) cider
   vinegar or rice wine vinegar
1 teaspoon sesame seeds
1 tablespoon sesame oil

1 Cut the pork into 2cm (¾ inch) cubes and place in a bowl. Put the remaining satay ingredients in a small bowl and whisk together. Pour over the pork and stir until well coated. Cover and leave to marinate in a cool place for at least 30 minutes or overnight.

2 To prepare the salad, halve the cucumber lengthways and scoop out the seeds with a teaspoon. Cut the cucumber into 2.5×1cm (1×½ inch) pieces and place in a colander. Sprinkle liberally with salt and leave for 30 minutes.

3 Rinse the cucumber under cold water and pat dry with absorbent kitchen paper. Mix the remaining salad ingredients together in a bowl, add the cucumber and turn until well coated. Cover and chill in the refrigerator until needed.

4 When ready to serve, preheat the grill to high. Thread the pork on to small (pre-soaked) bamboo skewers and grill for 3-4 minutes on each side, basting frequently. Serve immediately, garnished with spring onion (shallot) brushes and accompanied by the cucumber salad. *Serves 4.*

SPRING ONION (SHALLOT) BRUSHES: Feather the leafy ends with a knife and place in a bowl of iced water to open.

Index